FUN SONGS FOR CHILDREN'S CHURCH

PLAYBACK+
Speed • Pitch • Balance • Loop

To access audio visit:
www.halleonard.com/mylibrary

Enter Code
1664-5383-5681-5583

ISBN 978-1-5400-6475-2

HAL•LEONARD®

Visit Hal Leonard Online at
www.halleonard.com

Contact us:
Hal Leonard
7777 West Bluemound Road
Milwaukee, WI 53213
Email: info@halleonard.com

In Europe, contact:
Hal Leonard Europe Limited
42 Wigmore Street
Marylebone, London, W1U 2RN
Email: info@halleonardeurope.com

In Australia, contact:
Hal Leonard Australia Pty. Ltd.
4 Lentara Court
Cheltenham, Victoria, 3192 Australia
Email: info@halleonard.com.au

INTRODUCTION

This flexible resource is designed to help you lead songs for Children's Church, whether you play an instrument or not!

For non-musicians, simply sing along with the online backing tracks. (Pan right to hear the melody notes, pan left to mute them.) If you or another worker can play guitar, ukulele or keyboard, the songs may be performed either with or without the tracks. Older kids who play ukulele can strum along, too!

Keys have been carefully chosen for both singing and playing, but they can be changed using our exclusive **PLAYBACK+** online audio player. You can also speed up or slow down the tracks without altering the pitch. Setting loop points allows you to repeat a section as many times as you want! If streaming the tracks is inconvenient, you can download and burn them to a CD.

However you choose to use this book, the kids will enjoy learning and singing these time-tested songs!

CONTENTS

ALL NIGHT, ALL DAY

Spiritual

DEEP AND WIDE

Traditional

ARKY, ARKY

Traditional

Intro
Brightly

1. The

Verse

Lord ___ told No - ah, "There's gon - na be ___ a flood - y, flood - y."
(2.–5.) *See additional lyrics*

Lord ___ told No - ah, "There's gon - na be ___ a flood - y, flood - y.

Get those an - i - mals out of the mud - dy, mud - dy." Chil - dren of the

Chorus

Lord. So rise ___ and shine, __ and give God the glo - ry, glo - ry.

Additional Lyrics

2. The Lord told Noah to build him an arky, arky,
   Lord told Noah to build him an arky, arky,
   Build it out of gopher barky, barky,
   Children of the Lord.

3. The animals, the animals, they came in by twosies, twosies,
   Animals, the animals, they came in by twosies, twosies,
   Elephants and kangaroosies, roosies,
   Children of the Lord.

4. It rained and poured for forty daysies, daysies,
   Rained and poured for forty daysies, daysies.
   Almost drove those animals crazies, crazies,
   Children of the Lord.

5. The sun came out and dried up the landy, landy,
   (Look, there's the sun!) It dried up the landy, landy.
   Everything was fine and dandy, dandy,
   Children of the Lord.

DO LORD

Traditional

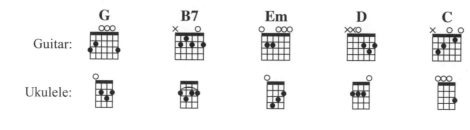

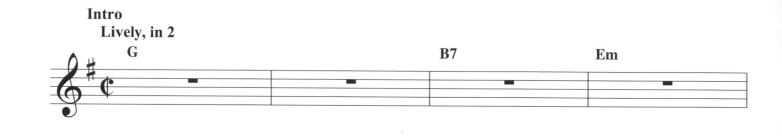

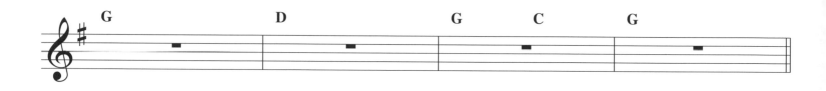

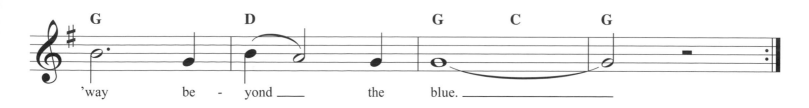

DOWN IN MY HEART

Traditional

GOD IS SO GOOD

Traditional

FATHER ABRAHAM

Traditional

Start a continuous motion with the right arm. Add a motion each time a new part of the body is mentioned.

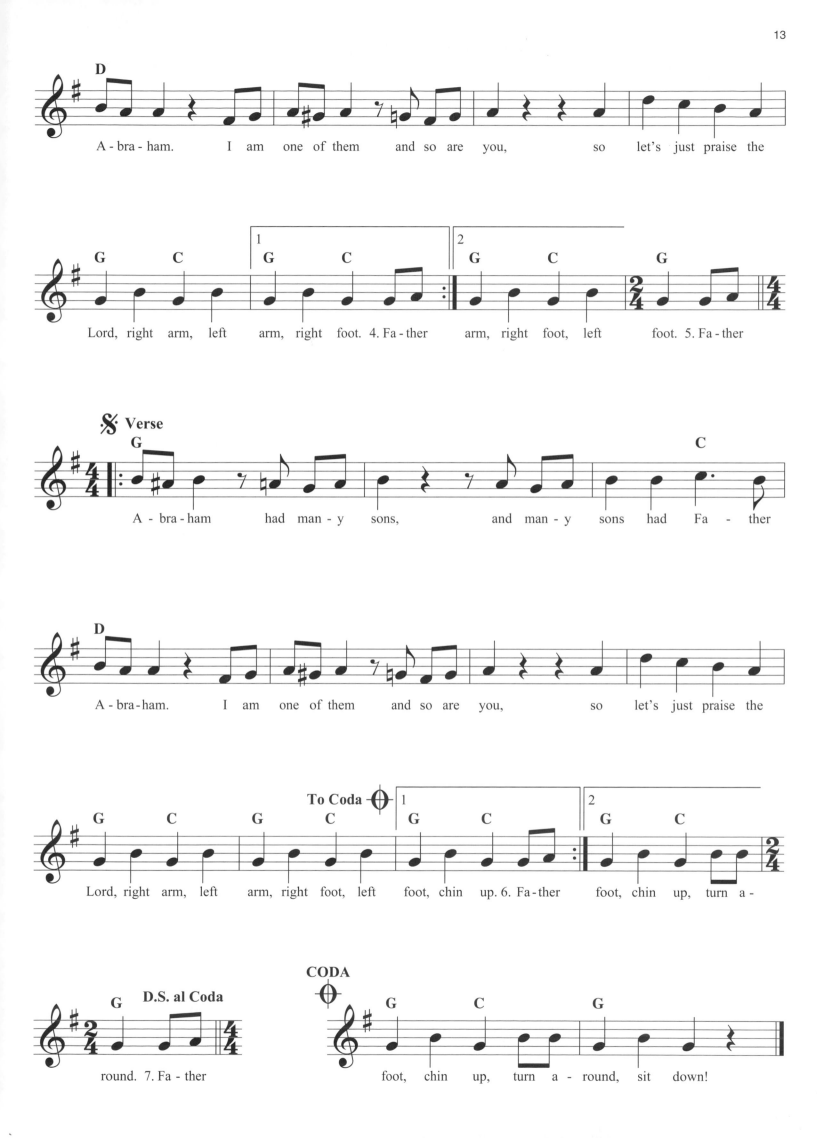

HALLELU, HALLELUJAH!

Traditional

I AM A C-H-R-I-S-T-I-A-N

Traditional

Guitar:

Ukulele:

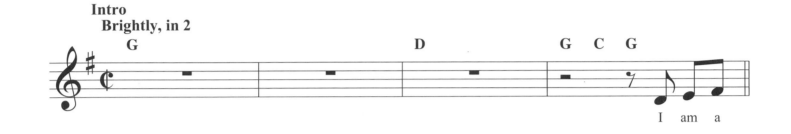

Intro
Brightly, in 2

I am a

Chorus

C,   I am a C-H,   I am a C-H-R-I-S-T-I-A-

N,   and I have C-H-R-I-S-T in my H-E-A-R-T and I will

L-I-V-E E-T-E-R-N-A-L-L-Y. I am a   N-A-L-L-Y.

Speed up on each repeat.

HE'S GOT THE WHOLE WORLD IN HIS HANDS

Traditional Spiritual

I'VE GOT PEACE LIKE A RIVER

Traditional

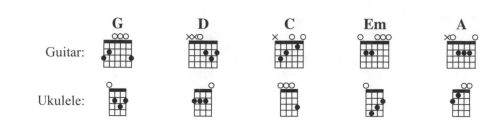

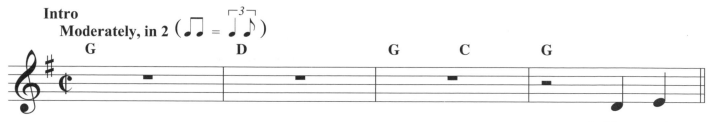

Intro
Moderately, in 2

1. I've got

Verse

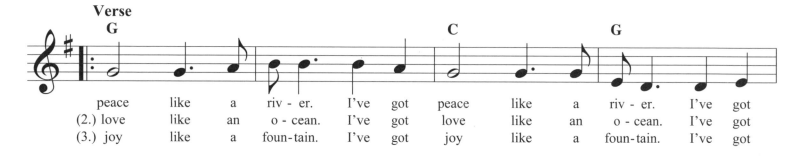

peace | like | a | riv - er. | I've got | peace | like | a | riv - er. | I've got
(2.) love | like | an | o - cean. | I've got | love | like | an | o - cean. | I've got
(3.) joy | like | a | foun-tain. | I've got | joy | like | a | foun-tain. | I've got

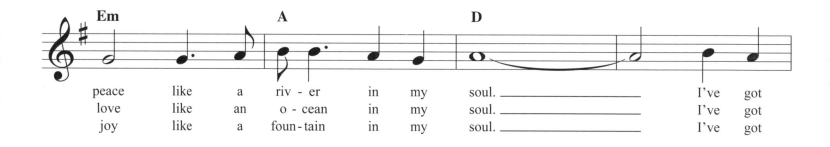

peace | like | a | riv - er | in | my | soul. _____ | I've got
love | like | an | o - cean | in | my | soul. _____ | I've got
joy | like | a | foun-tain | in | my | soul. _____ | I've got

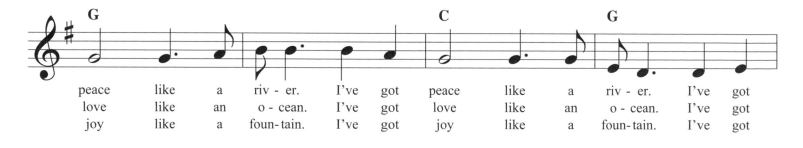

peace | like | a | riv - er. | I've got | peace | like | a | riv - er. | I've got
love | like | an | o - cean. | I've got | love | like | an | o - cean. | I've got
joy | like | a | foun-tain. | I've got | joy | like | a | foun-tain. | I've got

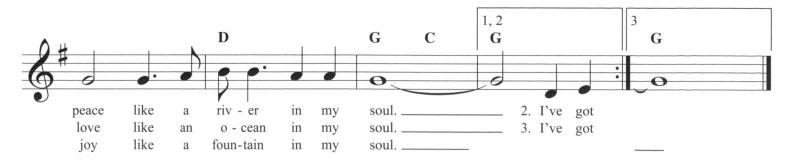

peace | like | a | riv - er | in | my | soul. _____ | 2. I've got
love | like | an | o - cean | in | my | soul. _____ | 3. I've got
joy | like | a | foun-tain | in | my | soul. _____

IF YOU'RE HAPPY AND YOU KNOW IT

Words and Music by L. Smith

Guitar: **C** **G** **D**

Ukulele:

Intro
Joyfully

C   G   D   G

1.–5. If you're

Verse

G   D   (clap, etc.)

hap - py   and   you   know   it,   { clap your hands. / stamp your foot. / nod your head. / turn a - round. / say A - men. }   If you're

G

hap - py   and   you   know   it,   { clap your hands. / stamp your foot. / nod your head. / turn a - round. / say A - men. }   If you're

C   G

hap - py   and   you   know   it,   then   your   face   will   sure - ly   show   it.   If you're

D   1.–4. G   5. G

hap - py   and   you   know   it,   { clap your hands. / stamp your foot. / nod your head. / turn a - round. / say A - }   If you're   men.

JESUS LOVES ME

Words by Anna B. Warner
Music by William B. Bradbury

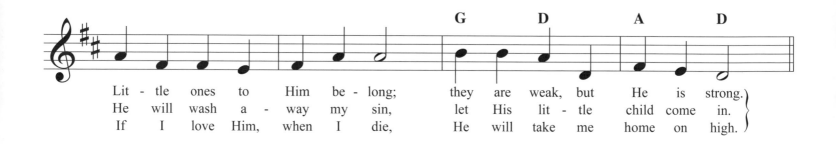

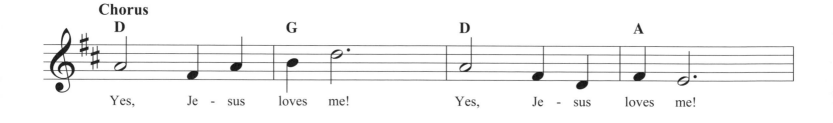

JESUS LOVES THE LITTLE CHILDREN

Words by Rev. C.H. Woolston
Music by George F. Root

LORD, I WANT TO BE A CHRISTIAN

Traditional Spiritual

MY GOD IS SO GREAT, SO STRONG AND SO MIGHTY

Traditional

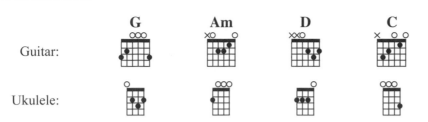

Intro
Confidently

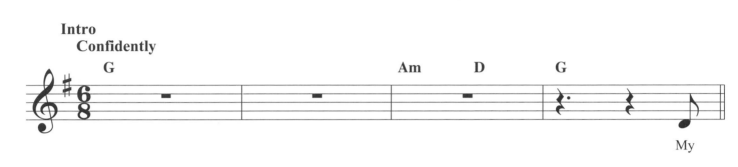

My

God is so great, so strong and so might-y! There's noth-ing my God can-not

do! My God is so great, so strong and so might-y! There's

noth-ing my God can-not do! The moun-tains are His, the

riv-ers are His, the stars are His hand-i-work, too. _____ My God is so great, so

strong and so might-y! There's noth-ing my God can-not do! My do!

OH, BE CAREFUL

Traditional

Additional Lyrics

2. Oh, be careful, little ears, what you hear.
   Oh, be careful, little ears, what you hear;
   For the Father up above is looking down in love,
   So be careful, little ears, what you hear.

3. Oh, be careful, little tongue, what you say.
   Oh, be careful, little tongue, what you say;
   For the Father up above is looking down in love,
   So be careful, little tongue, what you say.

4. Oh, be careful, little hands, what you do.
   Oh, be careful, little hands, what you do;
   For the Father up above is looking down in love,
   So be careful, little hands, what you do.

5. Oh, be careful, little feet, where you go.
   Oh, be careful, little feet, where you go;
   For the Father up above is looking down in love,
   So be careful, little feet, where you go.

PRAISE HIM, ALL YE LITTLE CHILDREN

Traditional Words
Music by Carey Bonner

REJOICE IN THE LORD ALWAYS

Words from Philippians 4:4
Traditional Music

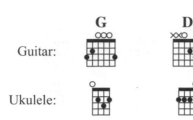

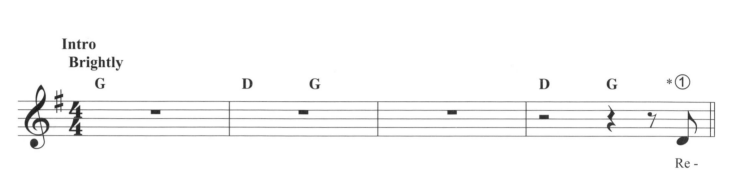

Intro
Brightly

Re-

Verse

joice in the Lord ___ al - ways, and a - gain I say, re - joice! Re -

joice in the Lord ___ al - ways, and a - gain I say, re - joice! Re -

Chorus

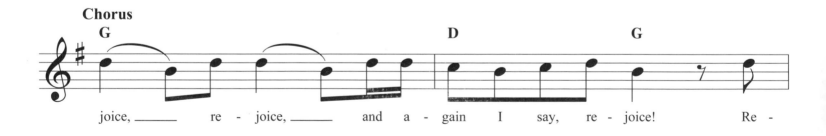

joice, ___ re - joice, ___ and a - gain I say, re - joice! Re -

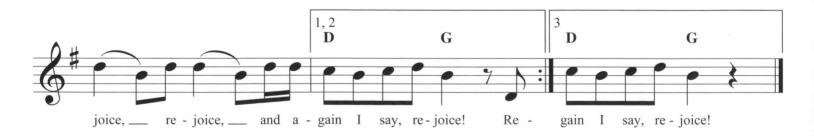

joice, ___ re - joice, ___ and a - gain I say, re - joice! Re - gain I say, re - joice!

* May be sung as a round.

ZACCHAEUS

Traditional

THIS LITTLE LIGHT OF MINE

Traditional

THE WISE MAN AND THE FOOLISH MAN

Traditional

Chorus

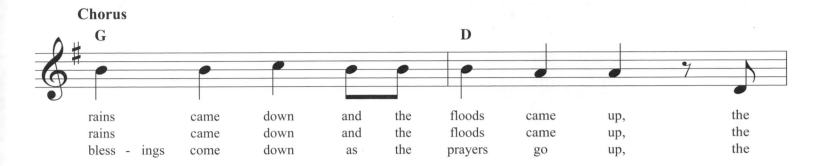

rains came down and the floods came up, the
rains came down and the floods came up, the
bless - ings come down as the prayers go up, the

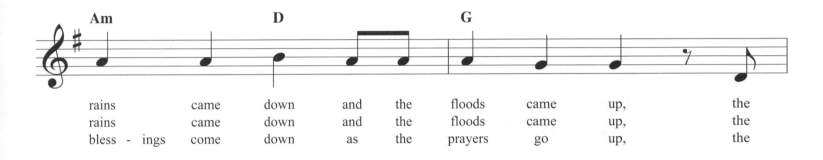

rains came down and the floods came up, the
rains came down and the floods came up, the
bless - ings come down as the prayers go up, the

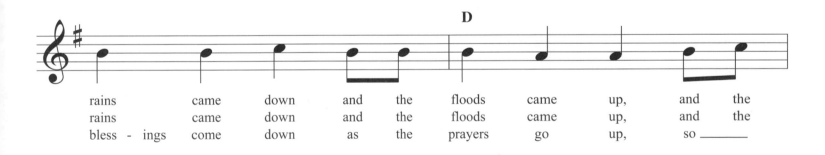

rains came down and the floods came up, and the
rains came down and the floods came up, and the
bless - ings come down as the prayers go up, so _____

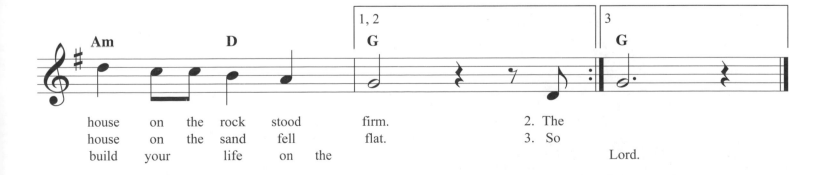

house on the rock stood firm. 2. The
house on the sand fell flat. 3. So
build your life on the Lord.

The BEST Easy Worship Songbooks

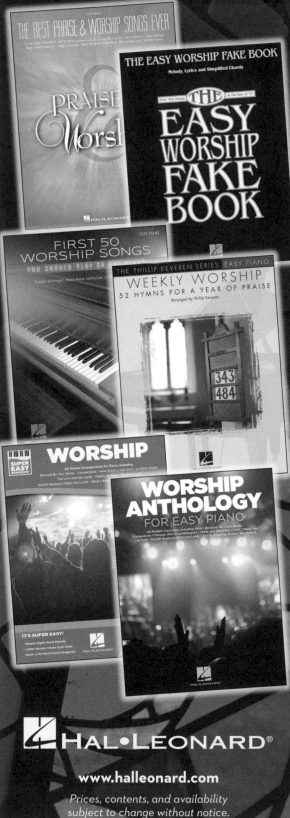

HAL•LEONARD®

www.halleonard.com

Prices, contents, and availability subject to change without notice.

THE BEST PRAISE & WORSHIP SONGS EVER

74 all-time favorites: Awesome God • Breathe • Days of Elijah • Here I Am to Worship • I Could Sing of Your Love Forever • Open the Eyes of My Heart • Shout to the Lord • We Bow Down • dozens more.
00311312 Easy Piano $19.99

THE EASY WORSHIP FAKE BOOK

This beginning fake book includes over 100 songs, all in the key of "C" with simplified chords. Songs include: Above All • Come, Now Is the Time to Worship • He Is Exalted • Lord, I Lift Your Name on High • You're Worthy of My Praise • and dozens more.
00240265 Melody/Lyrics/Chords $22.99

EASY WORSHIP MEDLEYS

The Phillip Keveren Series
20 favorites arranged into 10 easy piano medleys: Awesome Is the Lord Most High/Awesome God • Beautiful One/Oh Lord, You're Beautiful • Days of Elijah/Ancient of Days • Lord Most High/He Is Exalted • Once Again/There Is a Redeemer • and more.
00311997 Easy Piano $12.99

EVERLASTING GOD

The Phillip Keveren Series
18 worship songs masterfully arranged for beginning soloists by Phillip Keveren. Includes: Everlasting God • Forever Reign • Here I Am to Worship • How Great Is Our God • I Will Follow • Indescribable • Mighty to Save • Offering • Your Grace Is Enough • and more.
00102710 Beginning Piano Solo $10.99

FIRST 50 WORSHIP SONGS YOU SHOULD PLAY ON PIANO

50 worship favorites for beginning pianists: Blessed Be Your Name • Come, Now Is the Time to Worship • In Christ Alone • Lord, I Lift Your Name on High • Mighty to Save • Open the Eyes of My Heart • Shout to the Lord • 10,000 Reasons (Bless the Lord) • Thy Word • We Fall Down • Your Name • and many more.
00287138 Easy Piano $16.99

HERE I AM TO WORSHIP – FOR KIDS

This addition to the WorshipTogether series lets the kids join in on the best modern worship songs. Includes 20 favorites: Awesome God • Breathe • God of Wonders • He Is Exalted • Wonderful Maker • You Are My King (Amazing Love) • and more.
00316098 Easy Piano $15.99

THE HILLSONG WORSHIP COLLECTION

Easy piano arrangements of 20 worship favorites from this Australian music ministry. Includes: Came to My Rescue • Everyday • From the Inside Out • Hosanna • Lead Me to the Cross • Mighty to Save • Shout to the Lord • Worthy Is the Lamb • and more!
00312178 Easy Piano $14.99

MORE OF THE BEST PRAISE & WORSHIP SONGS EVER

76 contemporary worship favorites: Amazing Grace (My Chains Are Gone) • Blessed Be Your Name • Christ Is Risen • How Great Is Our God • Indescribable • Oh How He Loves You and Me • 10,000 Reasons (Bless the Lord) • What a Beautiful Name • and more.
00294444 Easy Piano $24.99

MORE OF THE EASY WORSHIP FAKE BOOK

Over 100 more contemporary worship favorites: Beautiful One • How He Loves • Jesus Messiah • Lead Me to the Cross • Revelation Song • You Never Let Go • Your Name • and more.
00240362 Melody/Lyrics/Chords $22.99

TIMELESS PRAISE

The Phillip Keveren Series
20 songs of worship: As the Deer • El Shaddai • Give Thanks • How Beautiful • How Majestic Is Your Name • Lord, I Lift Your Name on High • Shine, Jesus, Shine • There Is a Redeemer • Thy Word • and more.
00310712 Easy Piano $12.95

TODAY'S WORSHIP HITS

17 modern worship favorites, including: Forever Reign • How Great Is Our God • Our God • Sing to the King • 10,000 Reasons (Bless the Lord) and more.
00311439 Easy Piano $12.99

WEEKLY WORSHIP

The Phillip Keveren Series
52 hymns that will keep you playing all year long: Abide with Me • Be Thou My Vision • Holy, Holy, Holy • It Is Well with My Soul • Just As I Am • The Old Rugged Cross • Were You There? • and more.
00145342 Easy Piano $16.99

WORSHIP

60 super easy piano arrangements: Blessed Be Your Name • Cornerstone • How Great Is Our God • In Christ Alone • The Lion and the Lamb • Mighty to Save • Reckless Love • 10,000 Reasons (Bless the Lord) • What a Beautiful Name • Your Grace Is Enough • more.
00294871 Super Easy Songbook....................$14.99

WORSHIP ANTHOLOGY

40 worship favorites arranged at an easier level: Because He Lives, Amen • Great Are You Lord • Oceans (Where Feet May Fail) • Our God • 10,000 Reasons (Bless the Lord) • This Is Amazing Grace • and more.
00147947 Easy Piano $19.99

WORSHIP FAVORITES

20 powerful songs arranged for big-note piano: Above All • Forever • Here I Am to Worship • Open the Eyes of My Heart • Shout to the Lord • and dozens more.
00311207 Big-Note Piano............................$12.99